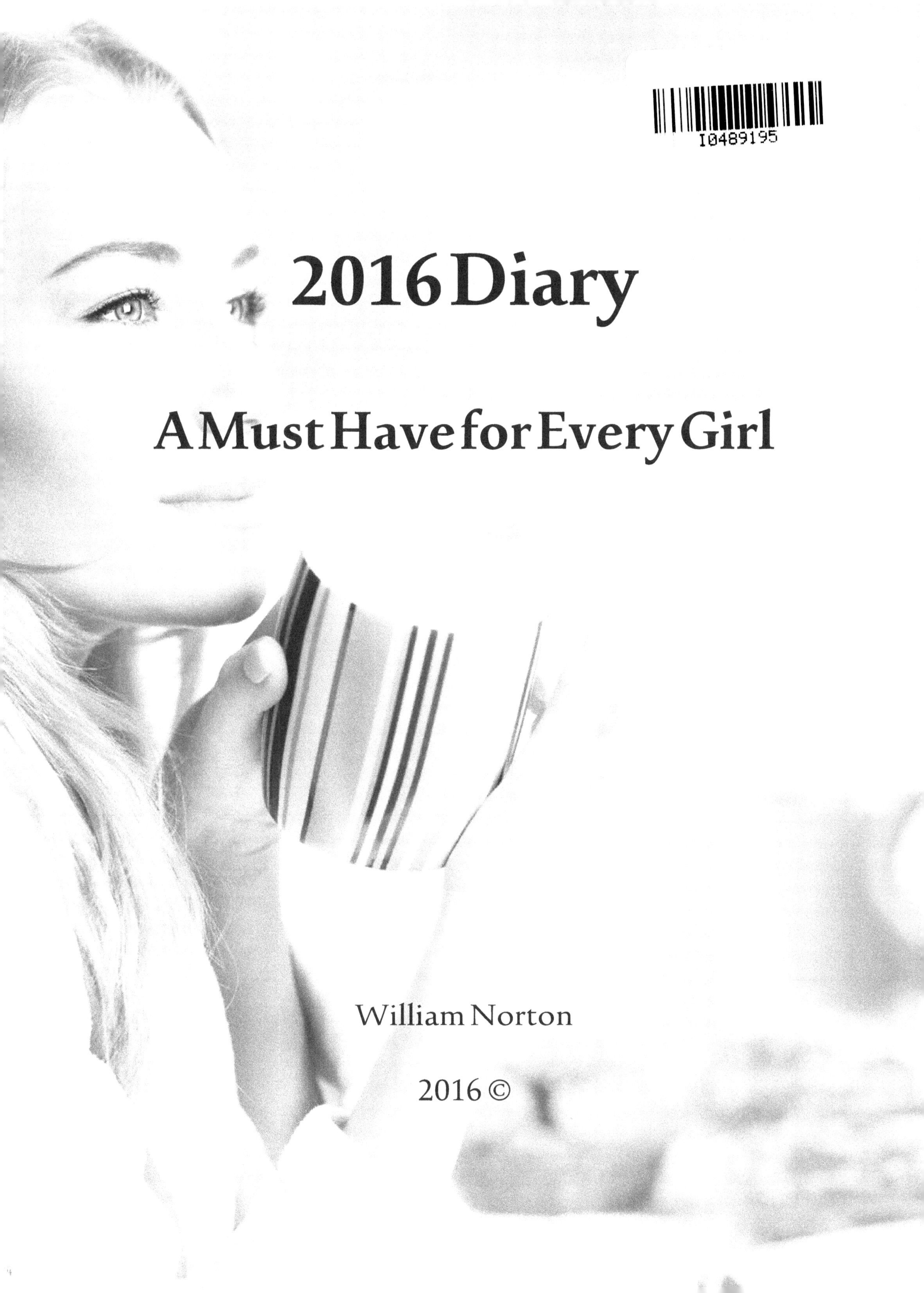

2016 Diary

A Must Have for Every Girl

William Norton

2016 ©

www.ingramcontent.com/pod-product-compliance
Lightning Source LLC
Chambersburg PA
CBHW080546190526
45169CB00007B/2655
* 9 7 8 1 5 3 0 1 1 1 6 2 6 *